Usborne

# All the Maths
## you need to know
## by age 7

Katie Daynes

Illustrated by Stefano Tognetti

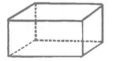

Designed by Alice Reese

Edited by Rosie Dickins

Series designer: Zoe Wray

Maths experts: Sheila Ebbutt and Penny Coltman

# Contents

Here's a list of the different topics covered.

The numbers tell you which pages to turn to.

Find out more about maths at Usborne Quicklinks.

For links to websites where you can watch videos about many of the topics in this book, and try simple online activities and puzzles, go to **usborne.com/Quicklinks** and type in the title of this book. Children should be supervised online.

We're maths bugs.

We'll help you to solve all kinds of problems.

You can look up what words mean in the glossary.

If you can't find what you're looking for here, try the index on page 80.

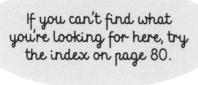

# What is maths?

Maths is all about **solving problems**.
Every day, we use **maths** in all kinds of ways.

Here are some examples.

NUMBERS

Counting

1 2 3 4 5 6 7 8

Is it odd or even?

+ − Adding & subtracting

Multiplying and dividing × ÷

PATTERNS

Are our patterns the same?

What shape of leaf comes next?

SHAPES

How many sides on each shape?

Do they fit together?

SIZES

Who is the longest, tallest, heaviest?

Here are some of the **tools** you can use to do maths.

Your **fingers!** They're very useful for counting.

Your **brain** is great at solving puzzles.

Can you count forwards AND backwards?

A **calculator** is a little computer that can do difficult **calculations**.

73 × 24

An **abacus** can help when you've run out of fingers.

**Scales** weigh how heavy something is.

8 g

A **ruler** measures how long, tall or wide something is.

14 + 28

For trickier problems, it helps to write down your workings out...

A **pencil** and some **paper**.

There are **many tricks** and **techniques** that make maths easier.

If you're counting lots of things, **tally marks** can be useful.

Mark a line for each thing.

For every 5th thing, put a line through the last 4 marks.

Two lots of five equals ten!

To **add** and **take away** numbers, you can use your fingers...

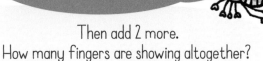

Start with the biggest number. Then there's less adding on to do!

What's seven add two?

Start with 7 fingers...

Then add 2 more. How many fingers are showing altogether?

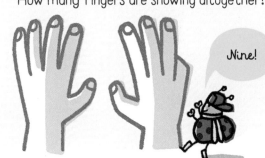

Nine!

What's eight take away five?

Start with 8 fingers...

Then fold down 5. How many fingers are left?

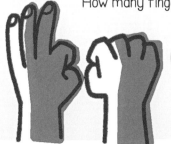

Three!

You'll find lots more helpful tips throughout this book.

# Numbers

The world is full of **numbers**. Think of all the places you **might** see them.

10:36

BK 5962 AC

63

19°C

How would we manage **WITHOUT** numbers?

JULY

21 My birthday!

This number tells you what page you're on.

Which numbers are important to you?

How old are you?

When were you born?

What's your address?

What's your favourite number?

We can write numbers down as **words, symbols** and even **patterns**.

This is how the numbers 1 to 6 appear on dice.

The numbers **zero** to **nine** each have their own symbol, called a **digit**.

The word digit comes from a very old word for finger!

That's because people have been using their fingers to count for thousands of years.

When you go higher than 9, you group things in tens...

...and count the extra ones.

I've counted one group of ten...

I've counted two extra ones.

The two digits go together to make a two-digit number.

Twelve!

9

# Numbers are either **even** or **odd**.

A number is even if it can be divided into two equal groups.

I've got 6 marbles.

We can have 3 each.

If a number CAN'T be divided into two equal groups, then it's odd.

I've got 7 berries.

I can have 4 and you can have 3.

As you count up in ones, the numbers go odd, even, odd, even... for as high as you can count.

ODD

EVEN

1 2 3 4 5 6 7 8 9 10

Numbers ending in 1, 3, 5, 7 or 9 are always odd.

Numbers ending in 2, 4, 6, 8 or 0 are always even.

Are these numbers odd or even?

52 78 75

ANSWER: 52 and 78 are even, 75 is odd.

When you count, you put numbers in **order** to make a **sequence**.

Numbers with a **lower value** come earlier in the sequence.

Which number comes after 8?

3 is one more than 2 and one less than 4.

9

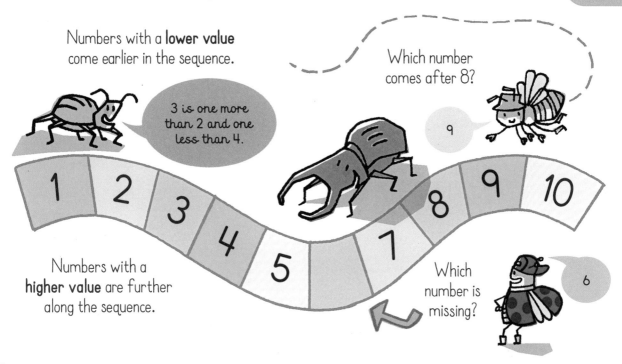

Numbers with a **higher value** are further along the sequence.

Which number is missing?

6

You can solve **many** maths problems by writing numbers in order on a line.

What's 4 **more** than 2?

6

What's 2 **less** than 17?

15

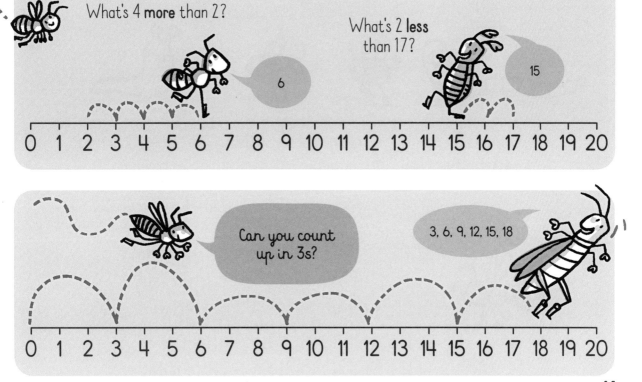

Can you count up in 3s?

3, 6, 9, 12, 15, 18

# Numbers can be very **BIG** or very small.

How many hairs do you have on your head? Is it a big number or a small one?

It's more than a hundred.

It's more than a thousand.

Is it less than a million?

People actually have roughly 100,000 (one hundred thousand) hairs.

What's the biggest number you know?

A billion.

A trillion.

What about a trillion and one?

However big the number you think of, you can always add one!

What's the smallest number you know?

One?

A quarter?

ZERO!

When **zero** is on its own, it means **nil** or **nothing**, but when it comes after other digits, it can **make the number MUCH bigger.**

Count how many zeroes you need for each of these numbers.

| | |
|---|---|
| 0 | ZERO |
| 10 | TEN |
| 100 | HUNDRED |
| 1,000 | THOUSAND |
| 1,000,000 | MILLION |
| 1,000,000,000 | BILLION |
| 1,000,000,000,000 | TRILLION |

# The bigger a number, the more digits it has.
# It's useful to imagine each digit in its own column.

This is the column for **hundreds**.

**Tens** go in this column...

...and **ones** go here.

Can you name the number in each **row**?

Eight.

Forty-eight.

Three hundred and forty-eight.

Write down three digits on separate pieces of paper. How many different numbers can you make by changing the order?

Try saying the numbers out loud.

Five hundred and twenty-one.

There are six different numbers! Which is the highest? Which is the lowest?

ANSWERS: 521 is the highest and 125 is the lowest.

# Adding and subtracting

You can solve lots of problems by **adding** or **subtracting** numbers.

Here's an example of **adding**.

How many petals are on these two flowers?

Count up the **total** number of petals.

It's quickest to start with the bigger number and count on from there.

Three on this flower...

...and **seven** on this one.

I'll start with seven and count on three. Eight... nine... ten. The answer is **ten!**

Here's an example of **subtracting**.

Something smells good!

I've baked ten cookies!

I'll take these four...

How many cookies are left?

Only **six!**

14

Maths uses symbols as a short way to write down problems.

The plus sign means 'add'.

Plus

The minus sign means 'take away', or 'subtract'.

Minus

Equals means 'has the same value as'.

Equals

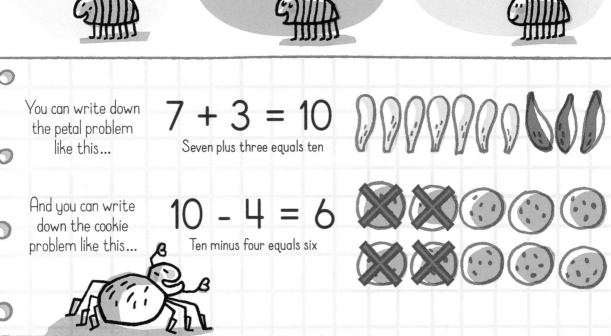

You can write down the petal problem like this...

## 7 + 3 = 10
Seven plus three equals ten

And you can write down the cookie problem like this...

## 10 - 4 = 6
Ten minus four equals six

How would you write down these problems using symbols?

**A** Beetle makes **ten** sandcastles.

Then I make **four** more.

Now there are **fourteen** sandcastles.

**B** Caterpillar has **eleven** crayons.

I give **three** to my friend.

Now he only has **eight** crayons.

ANSWERS: A. 10 + 4 = 14, B. 11 - 3 = 8

# Writing numbers in order can help you to add and subtract.

Here's how you can add and subtract using a **number track**.

5 + 3 =

Start at 5 and count on 3.

The answer is 8.
5 + 3 = 8

8

8 - 3 =

Start at 8 and count back 3.

The answer is 5.
8 - 3 = 5

5

Another way to subtract is to find the **difference** between two numbers.

I can jump 7 cm.

I can jump 9 cm.

What's the difference between the two jumps?

2 cm.

Here's how you can write it as a subtraction.

9 - 7 = 2

You can also write it as an addition...
7 + 2 = 9

When you add and subtract using the same numbers,
you make a group of related facts - known as a **fact family**.

A fact is something that is true.
1 + 5 = 6 is an addition fact.

Let's look at the fact family for the numbers 7, 2 and 9.

There are two addition facts...

The biggest number is the answer.

The numbers you're adding can swap places.

...and two subtraction facts.

For subtraction, start with the biggest number.

The number you subtract and the answer can swap places.

Here are the additions and subtractions
that make up another fact family.

Which numbers are missing?

6 + 7 = 13

☆ + 6 = ☆

13 - 6 = ☆

☆ - ☆ = 6

Can you see how 7, 2 and 9
work together in these facts?

20 + 70 = 90

The more maths you do, the more patterns you'll spot.

900 - 700 = 200

ANSWERS: 7 + 6 = 13, 13 - 6 = 7, 13 = 6 + 7, 6 = 7 - 13

17

**Number bonds** are pairs of numbers that add up to the same total. Learning them makes it easier to do maths in your head.

Here are the number bonds to 10.

1 + 9   2 + 8   3 + 7   4 + 6

= 10

5 + 5

9 + 1   8 + 2   7 + 3   6 + 4

The number bonds on my side are the same as the ones on your side.

Mine are just the other way around.

Recognizing number bonds can help you to do longer sums.

2 + 8 + 5 =

I know that 2 + 8 = 10, so I just need to work out 10 + 5.

The answer is 15.

Number bonds can also help you to subtract.

10 - 9 =

1

I know which number goes with 9 to make 10.

10 11 12 13 14 15

Which numbers are missing in these puzzles?

10 - ☆ = 7

10 - ☆ = 4

ANSWERS: 10 - 3 = 7, 10 - 6 = 4

18

**If you know the number bonds to 10, it's easy to make bonds to 20.**

You just take the number bond to 10...

$$1 + 9$$

...and add another 10.

$$+ \quad 10$$

You can either add the 10 to the first number...

$$11 + 9 = 20$$

$$1 + 19 = 20$$

...or to the second number.

Here are some of the number bonds to 100.

| | | |
|---|---|---|
| 10 + 90 | 40 + 60 | 70 + 30 |
| 20 + 80 | 50 + 50 | 80 + 20 |
| 30 + 70 | 60 + 40 | 90 + 10 |

Do they look familiar?

80 + 20 is similar to 8 + 2...

Can you count up in tens? And back down in tens?

We've made a tens number line!

One hundred, ninety, eighty, seventy...

+10  +10  +10  +10          −10   −10   −10

| 0 | 10 | 20 | 30 | 40 | 50 | 60 | 70 | 80 | 90 | 100 |
|---|----|----|----|----|----|----|----|----|----|-----|
| Zero | Ten | Twenty | Thirty | Forty | Fifty | Sixty | Seventy | Eighty | Ninety | One hundred |

19

**Another way to make maths easier is by rounding numbers up or down.**

Ten is a good number to use, because it's easy to add or subtract ten.

I'm 7 today. In 10 years time I'll be 17.

7 + 10 = 17

Here's an example of rounding up to 10.

Nine is one **less** than ten. So, to add nine you can add ten, then subtract one.

9 = 10 - 1

27 + 9    is the same as    27 + 10 - 1

Add the ten.    27 + 10 = 37

37 - 1    Subtract the one.

= 36    And the answer is thirty-six.

And here's an example of rounding down to 10.

Eleven is one **more** than ten. So, to subtract eleven you can subtract ten, then subtract one more.

11 = 10 + 1

27 - 11    is the same as    27 - 10 + 1

I'll subtract the ten then subtract the one.

17 - 1    = 16

Ooh, clever!

Try using number bonds and rounding to solve these problems.

We've been travelling for 11 minutes.

We'll arrive in 10 minutes.

Can you work them out in your head?

My Great-gran will be 100 in 11 years time.

How long will their whole journey take?

10 + 10 = 20
20 + 1 = <u>21</u>

How old is Great-gran now?

100 - 10 = 90
90 - 1 = <u>89</u>

I've got 29 coins...

And I've got 70 coins...

I have 28 buttons and I need 11 to mend my coat.

How many coins have they got altogether?

30 + 70 = 100
100 - 1 = <u>99</u>

How many buttons will bug have left?

28 - 10 = 18
18 - 1 = <u>17</u>

## What happens when you add or subtract zero?

20 + 0 = 20

100 - 0 = 100

Nothing!

You're adding and subtracting nothing...

...so the number stays the same.

**+ -**

When you're adding numbers, it can help to add up to the nearest ten, then add on from there. It's called **bridging** and it works like this...

This bus has 10 passenger seats on each deck.

The bugs getting on need to fill up the bottom deck first, before going onto the top deck.

2 of us would fill up the bottom deck...

So that leaves 3 of us to go on the top deck.

How many passenger bugs are there altogether?

$8 + 5$ which is the same as $8 + 2 + 3$ and can become $10 + 3 = 13$

You can also use a **number line** to work out sums using bridging.

For 8 + 5, start by putting 8 on the line...

I can add 2 to reach 10.

But we need to add 5...

...so let's add 3 more.

Ta dah! The answer is 13.

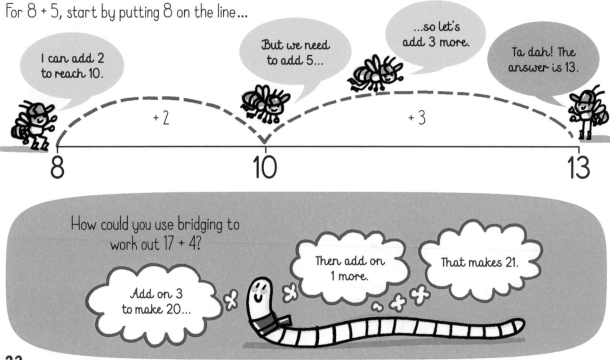

+ 2

+ 3

8          10          13

How could you use bridging to work out 17 + 4?

Add on 3 to make 20...

Then add on 1 more.

That makes 21.

If you're adding on a two-digit number, try splitting it up into tens and ones first. This is called **partitioning**.

Let's have a go at partitioning the number 23.

23

How many tens is it made up of?

Two!

2  3

And how many ones?

Three!

You can also write this as... 20 + 3

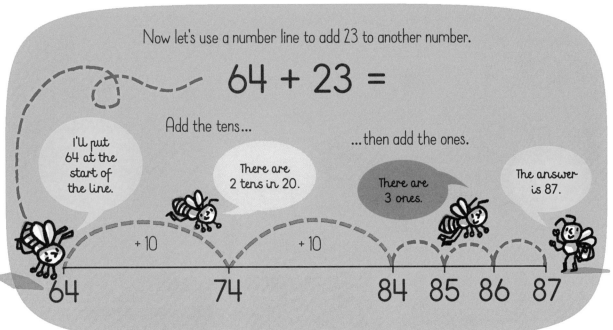

Now let's use a number line to add 23 to another number.

64 + 23 =

Add the tens...

...then add the ones.

I'll put 64 at the start of the line.

There are 2 tens in 20.

There are 3 ones.

The answer is 87.

+ 10          + 10

64          74          84  85  86  87

Can you imagine a number line and do these sums in your head?

43 + 14 = ☆     68 + 11 = ☆

Maths you do in your head is known as **mental maths**.

ANSWERS: 43 + 14 = 57, 68 + 11 = 79

23

# You can also use a number line to subtract a two-digit number.

## 73 - 14 =

First partition the number you're subtracting into tens and ones.

Easy! That's 1 ten...

...and 4 ones.

Then put the big number on the far right of the number line and work back from there.

Subtract the tens, then subtract the ones.

I've got 1 ten to take away.

I'll take away the 4 ones.

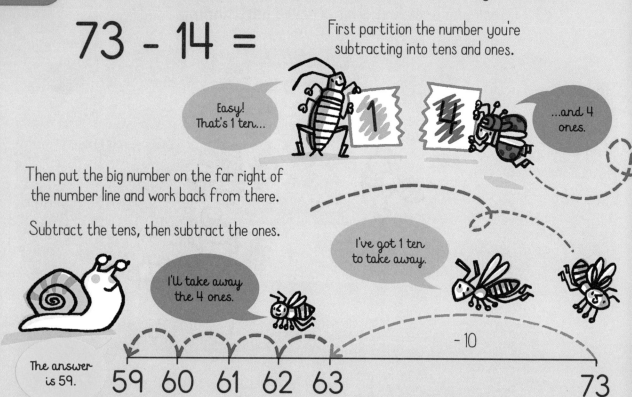

- 10

The answer is 59.

59  60  61  62  63                               73

---

## If you partition **both** numbers, you can add the tens and ones separately.

34 becomes 30 and 4, and 12 becomes 10 and 2.

## 34 + 12

This is called the expanded column method.

I'll add up the tens.

I'll add up the ones.

+  (3 0)  (4)
   (1 0)  (2)

30 + 10 = 40

4 + 2 = 6

= 4 0 + 6

And I'll add both answers together.

= 46

24

You can use expanded columns for subtractions as well.

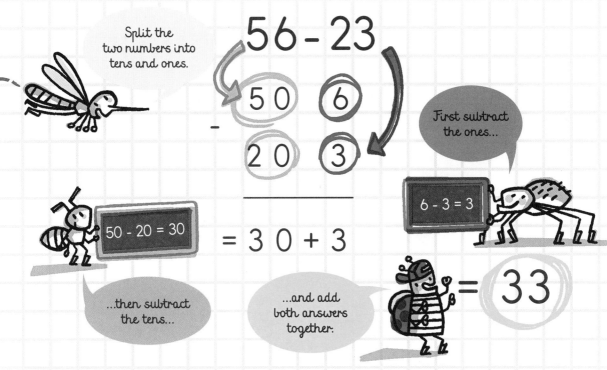

Split the two numbers into tens and ones.

$$56 - 23$$

First subtract the ones...

6 - 3 = 3

50 - 20 = 30

$$= 30 + 3$$

...then subtract the tens...

...and add both answers together.

$$= 33$$

The same addition and subtraction puzzles can also be written out like this...

Line the numbers up below each other, so the tens and ones are in the correct columns.

It's called the **column** method.

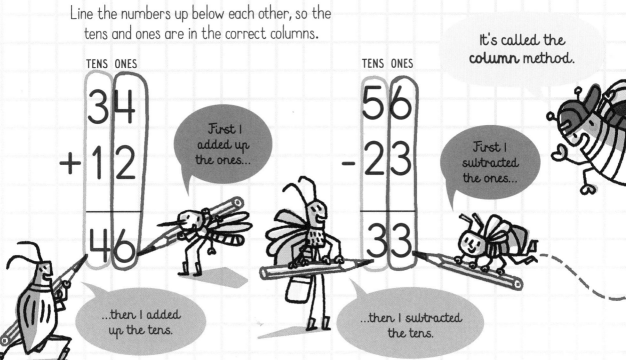

TENS ONES

$$\begin{array}{r} 34 \\ + 12 \\ \hline 46 \end{array}$$

First I added up the ones...

...then I added up the tens.

TENS ONES

$$\begin{array}{r} 56 \\ - 23 \\ \hline 33 \end{array}$$

First I subtracted the ones...

...then I subtracted the tens.

25

# Another way to add and subtract tens and ones is with a **hundred square**.

To add on a ten, move down one square. To add on a one, move right one square.
To subtract, do the opposite (move up for tens and left for ones).

Here's how it works for 23 + 56.

+ 10 ⬇    + 1 ⬆➡

| 1 | 2 | 3 | 4 | 5 | 6 | 7 | 8 | 9 | 10 |
|---|---|---|---|---|---|---|---|---|---|
| 11 | 12 | 13 | 14 | 15 | 16 | 17 | 18 | 19 | 20 |
| 21 | 22 | 23 | 24 | 25 | 26 | 27 | 28 | 29 | 30 |
| 31 | 32 | 33 | 34 | 35 | 36 | 37 | 38 | 39 | 40 |
| 41 | 42 | 43 | 44 | 45 | 46 | 47 | 48 | 49 | 50 |
| 51 | 52 | 53 | 54 | 55 | 56 | 57 | 58 | 59 | 60 |
| 61 | 62 | 63 | 64 | 65 | 66 | 67 | 68 | 69 | 70 |
| 71 | 72 | 73 | 74 | 75 | 76 | 77 | 78 | 79 | 80 |
| 81 | 82 | 83 | 84 | 85 | 86 | 87 | 88 | 89 | 90 |
| 91 | 92 | 93 | 94 | 95 | 96 | 97 | 98 | 99 | 100 |

The answer is 79.

Can you work out the answers to these problems?

**A**

$5 + 4 =$

**B**

$2 + 8 =$

Look out for number bonds.

**C**

$20 - 3 =$

**D**

$300 - 200 =$

Which ones can you do in your head?

It's the same as 3 - 2 but with hundreds...

**E**

$72 - 0 =$

$40 + 11 =$ **F**

I'll start by adding on 10...

**G**

$55 + 34 =$

I'll partition the tens and ones.

**H**

$88 - 43 =$

I think I'll use the hundred square.

27

# Multiplying...

Multiplying a number is the same as adding it lots of times.

How many bugs are there on the leaves?

There are 2 of us on each leaf...

...and 4 leaves altogether.

You can find the answer by adding up 4 lots of 2.

$$2 + 2 + 2 + 2 = 8$$

Or you can write the calculation as a multiplication.

This is the symbol for 'lots of', 'multiply', or 'times'.

Two multiplied by four equals eight

$$2 \times 4 = 8$$

The numbers that are multiplied are called **factors**.

The answer is called the **product**.

When something multiplies in size, it gets bigger.

Caterpillar's knitting is **twice** as long as spider's.

I've only knitted 4 stripes...

How many stripes has caterpillar knitted?

I've knitted 8.

$$4 \times 2 = 8$$

Four multiplied by two equals eight

28

# ...and dividing

When you divide a number, you split it up into equal amounts.

One form of dividing is **sharing fairly**.

How can I share 8 grapes between 4 friends?

Give us 2 each.

Then they're shared **equally**, with none left over.

Another form of dividing is **subtracting** the same number lots of times.

I have 8 seeds and I want to plant 4 in each pot.

To work out how many pots bee needs, start with 8 and subtract 4 until you reach 0.

$$8 - 4 - 4 = 0$$

Subtracting 2 lots of 4 makes 0.

That means bug needs 2 pots.

Here's how you write both these examples down as a division.

This is the symbol for dividing.

Eight divided by four equals two

$$8 ÷ 4 = 2$$

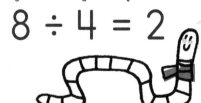

You could also say '8 shared between 4 is 2 each'.

# You can swap the numbers in a multiplication question, and the answer will stay the same.

How many cupcakes are there altogether?

There are 3 in a column and 4 columns...

$3 \times 4 = 12$

There are 4 in a row and 3 rows...

$4 \times 3 = 12$

Either way makes 12.

# You can't swap over the numbers in a division question. But you can swap the number you're dividing by with the answer.

Share out 12 cupcakes so there are 3 on a plate. How many plates do you need?

$12 \div 3 = 4$

Four.

Share 12 cupcakes onto 4 plates. How many cupcakes are on each plate?

$12 \div 4 = 3$

Three.

The puzzles on this page all use the same three numbers.

Together, the puzzles make a multiplying and dividing fact family.

$3 \times 4 = 12$     $12 \div 4 = 3$

$4 \times 3 = 12$     $12 \div 3 = 4$

# Dividing is the opposite of multiplying.

6 leaves shared between 3 caterpillars gives them 2 each.

$6 \div 3 = 2$

3 caterpillars with 2 leaves each makes 6 leaves in total.

$3 \times 2 = 6$

## If you multiply or divide a number by one, it stays the same.

I've bought a four-pack of peaches. How many peaches do I have?

Four!

$4 \times 1 = 4$

If I only share my sweets with myself, then I can eat ALL of them!

$10 \div 1 = 10$

But you'll be sick.

And we'll be sad.

If you multiply something by zero, you always end up with zero.

There are 6 eggs in a box.

How many eggs are there in zero boxes?

None!

BOXES OF EGGS

SOLD OUT

$6 \times 0 = 0$

Don't even try to divide something by zero - it's impossible!

There's no one here to share the coconuts, so they can't be shared!

31

# You can use a number line to work out a multiplication.

Every leap on this number line adds on **five**.

To work out 5 × 2, take 2 leaps along the line.

5 × 2 = 10

0  1 2 3 4  5  6 7 8 9  10    15    20    25

5 × 1     5 × 2     5 × 3          5 × 5

To work out 5 × 4, leap along the line 4 times.

5 × 4 = 20

Let's use the number line to work out this problem.

I eat 5 pieces of fruit and veg a day.

How many pieces of fruit or veg does caterpillar eat in a week?

There are 7 days in a week...

5 times 7 is 35.

5 × 7 = 35

Try working out these puzzles.

**A** 5 × 10 = ☆     **B** 5 × 5 = ☆

# You can use the same number line for dividing.

For example, to find out 35 ÷ 5 you need to
work out how many times 5 goes into 35.

You can do this by seeing how many leaps
of five it takes to reach 35.

It takes
7 leaps!

35 ÷ 5 = 7

| 30 | 35 | 40 | 45 | 50 |
|---|---|---|---|---|
| 5 × 6 | 5 × 7 | 5 × 8 | 5 × 9 | 5 × 10 |

Caterpillar has 45 pieces of fruit and veg.
If he keeps eating 5 a day, how many days will they last?

Let's look on
the number line.

45 is 5 × 9.

So it will last
him 9 days.

How would you write
this as a division?

45 ÷ 5 = 9

**C** 15 ÷ 5 = ☆    **D** 30 ÷ 5 = ☆

ANSWERS: A. 50, B. 25, C. 3, D. 6

33

# When you multiply any number by two, you **double** its value.

There are 6 seeds in a packet.

How many seeds are there in two packets?

6 × 2 = 12

Double the number!

Twice as many!

# When you divide a number by two, you **halve** its value.

The recipe says 4 eggs.

We're only making half the amount. How many eggs do we need?

× 4

4 ÷ 2 = 2

Half of 4.

Halving is the opposite of doubling.

# Here are some doubling and halving facts for even and odd numbers.

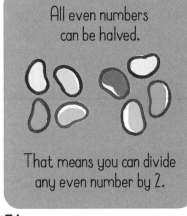

All even numbers can be halved.

That means you can divide any even number by 2.

You can't halve an odd number of things...

...unless you cut one of them in half!

When you double an odd number...

...you always end up with an even number.

# A **times table** (or multiplication table) is a list of multiplications for the same number.

Here is the times table for 2. It's called the 2 times table.

You can also write the factors the other way round.

$3 \times 2 = 6$

$4 \times 2 = 8$

FACTORS → PRODUCT

$2 \times 1 = 2$
$2 \times 2 = 4$
$2 \times 3 = 6$
$2 \times 4 = 8$
$2 \times 5 = 10$
$2 \times 6 = 12$
$2 \times 7 = 14$
$2 \times 8 = 16$
$2 \times 9 = 18$
$2 \times 10 = 20$
$2 \times 11 = 22$
$2 \times 12 = 24$

The product numbers go up in leaps of 2.

The products in the 2 times table are known as the family of 2.

Times tables help with multiplication AND division.

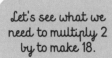

What's 18 divided by 2?

Let's see what we need to multiply 2 by to make 18.

The answer is 9.

There are different chants you can say to help you remember the 2 times table.

One two is two, two twos are four...

Or simply...

Two, four, six, eight...

## Knowing times tables by heart helps with many maths puzzles.

How many wheels are there on 9 bicycles?

How many pairs of socks can you make from 22 odd socks?

ANSWERS: 18 wheels, 11 pairs of socks.

35

# Take a look at the times table for the number 5.

Can you see any patterns?

## 5 ×

| | | | |
|---|---|---|---|
| 5 | × 1 | = | 5 |
| 5 | × 2 | = | 10 |
| 5 | × 3 | = | 15 |
| 5 | × 4 | = | 20 |
| 5 | × 5 | = | 25 |
| 5 | × 6 | = | 30 |
| 5 | × 7 | = | 35 |
| 5 | × 8 | = | 40 |
| 5 | × 9 | = | 45 |
| 5 | × 10 | = | 50 |
| 5 | × 11 | = | 55 |
| 5 | × 12 | = | 60 |

The products end in 5, then 0, then 5, then 0...

Each product is 5 more than the one before it...

+ 5

- 5

...and 5 less than the one after it.

If there are 5 bananas in a bunch, how many bananas are there in 6 bunches?

× 6

Try counting up in fives, using your fingers.

10  15  20

5

25  30

There are 30 bananas!

Turn the page to find all the times tables from 1 to 12.

A clock face is divided up into 12 lots of 5.

What's 5 x 12? I'll look at the 5 times table.

5 × 12 = 60

Turn to page 59 to learn about telling the time.

5

10

I'm counting around in fives.

A  What number will bee have counted to when she lands on the 7?

B  When bee has counted to 50, where will she be on the clock?

ANSWERS: A, 35, B, on the 10.

# The 10 times table is easy to remember.

× ÷

| 10 × | | | |
|------|---|---|---|
| 10 × 1 | = | 10 |
| 10 × 2 | = | 20 |
| 10 × 3 | = | 30 |
| 10 × 4 | = | 40 |
| 10 × 5 | = | 50 |
| 10 × 6 | = | 60 |
| 10 × 7 | = | 70 |
| 10 × 8 | = | 80 |
| 10 × 9 | = | 90 |
| 10 × 10 | = | 100 |
| 10 × 11 | = | 110 |
| 10 × 12 | = | 120 |

To times by 10, you add a zero on the end!

Let's take a closer look at what's happening.

When you multiply a single-digit number by 10, it moves into the tens column... and you put a 0 in the ones column.

TENS ONES

$$\begin{array}{cc} 1 & 0 \\ \times & 4 \\ \hline = 4 & 0 \end{array}$$

What happens when you multiply a two-digit number by 10?

The digit in the tens column moves into the hundreds column.

HUNDREDS TENS ONES

$$\begin{array}{ccc} & 1 & 0 \\ \times & 1 & 2 \\ \hline = 1 & 2 & 0 \end{array}$$

The digit in the ones column moves into the tens column.

And a zero goes in the ones column.

If each token is worth 10 points, how many points does ladybird have?

$10 \times 7 = 70$

There are 10 stickers in a pack.

I need 30 stickers. How many packs do I need?

$10 \times ? = 30$
$30 \div 10 = 3$

You need 3 packs!

On a centimetre ruler, each centimetre is divided into 10 millimetres.

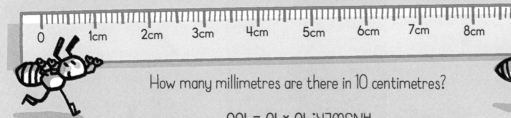

0    1cm    2cm    3cm    4cm    5cm    6cm    7cm    8cm    9cm    10cm

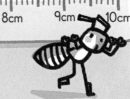

How many millimetres are there in 10 centimetres?

ANSWER: 10 × 10 = 100

37

# Here are all the times tables from 1 to 12.

Try learning them off by heart.

## 1 ×

| | | | |
|---|---|---|---|
| 1 × 1 | = | 1 |
| 1 × 2 | = | 2 |
| 1 × 3 | = | 3 |
| 1 × 4 | = | 4 |
| 1 × 5 | = | 5 |
| 1 × 6 | = | 6 |
| 1 × 7 | = | 7 |
| 1 × 8 | = | 8 |
| 1 × 9 | = | 9 |
| 1 × 10 | = | 10 |
| 1 × 11 | = | 11 |
| 1 × 12 | = | 12 |

## 2 ×

| | | | |
|---|---|---|---|
| 2 × 1 | = | 2 |
| 2 × 2 | = | 4 |
| 2 × 3 | = | 6 |
| 2 × 4 | = | 8 |
| 2 × 5 | = | 10 |
| 2 × 6 | = | 12 |
| 2 × 7 | = | 14 |
| 2 × 8 | = | 16 |
| 2 × 9 | = | 18 |
| 2 × 10 | = | 20 |
| 2 × 11 | = | 22 |
| 2 × 12 | = | 24 |

## 3 ×

| | | | |
|---|---|---|---|
| 3 × 1 | = | 3 |
| 3 × 2 | = | 6 |
| 3 × 3 | = | 9 |
| 3 × 4 | = | 12 |
| 3 × 5 | = | 15 |
| 3 × 6 | = | 18 |
| 3 × 7 | = | 21 |
| 3 × 8 | = | 24 |
| 3 × 9 | = | 27 |
| 3 × 10 | = | 30 |
| 3 × 11 | = | 33 |
| 3 × 12 | = | 36 |

The 4 times table is double the 2 times table.

The 6 times table is double the 3 times table.

## 4 ×

| | | | |
|---|---|---|---|
| 4 × 1 | = | 4 |
| 4 × 2 | = | 8 |
| 4 × 3 | = | 12 |
| 4 × 4 | = | 16 |
| 4 × 5 | = | 20 |
| 4 × 6 | = | 24 |
| 4 × 7 | = | 28 |
| 4 × 8 | = | 32 |
| 4 × 9 | = | 36 |
| 4 × 10 | = | 40 |
| 4 × 11 | = | 44 |
| 4 × 12 | = | 48 |

## 5 ×

| | | | |
|---|---|---|---|
| 5 × 1 | = | 5 |
| 5 × 2 | = | 10 |
| 5 × 3 | = | 15 |
| 5 × 4 | = | 20 |
| 5 × 5 | = | 25 |
| 5 × 6 | = | 30 |
| 5 × 7 | = | 35 |
| 5 × 8 | = | 40 |
| 5 × 9 | = | 45 |
| 5 × 10 | = | 50 |
| 5 × 11 | = | 55 |
| 5 × 12 | = | 60 |

## 6 ×

| | | | |
|---|---|---|---|
| 6 × 1 | = | 6 |
| 6 × 2 | = | 12 |
| 6 × 3 | = | 18 |
| 6 × 4 | = | 24 |
| 6 × 5 | = | 30 |
| 6 × 6 | = | 36 |
| 6 × 7 | = | 42 |
| 6 × 8 | = | 48 |
| 6 × 9 | = | 54 |
| 6 × 10 | = | 60 |
| 6 × 11 | = | 66 |
| 6 × 12 | = | 72 |

Knowing your times tables will help you with all kinds of maths puzzles.

**The 8 times table is double the 4 times table.**

**Can you see a pattern in the 9 times table?**

## 7 ×

7 × 1 = 7
7 × 2 = 14
7 × 3 = 21
7 × 4 = 28
7 × 5 = 35
7 × 6 = 42
7 × 7 = 49
7 × 8 = 56
7 × 9 = 63
7 × 10 = 70
7 × 11 = 77
7 × 12 = 84

## 8 ×

8 × 1 = 8
8 × 2 = 16
8 × 3 = 24
8 × 4 = 32
8 × 5 = 40
8 × 6 = 48
8 × 7 = 56
8 × 8 = 64
8 × 9 = 72
8 × 10 = 80
8 × 11 = 88
8 × 12 = 96

## 9 ×

9 × 1 = 9
9 × 2 = 18
9 × 3 = 27
9 × 4 = 36
9 × 5 = 45
9 × 6 = 54
9 × 7 = 63
9 × 8 = 72
9 × 9 = 81
9 × 10 = 90
9 × 11 = 99
9 × 12 = 108

**The 10 times table is double the 5 times table.**

**Can you see a pattern in the 11 times table?**

**The 12 times table is double the 6 times table.**

## 10 ×

10 × 1 = 10
10 × 2 = 20
10 × 3 = 30
10 × 4 = 40
10 × 5 = 50
10 × 6 = 60
10 × 7 = 70
10 × 8 = 80
10 × 9 = 90
10 × 10 = 100
10 × 11 = 110
10 × 12 = 120

## 11 ×

11 × 1 = 11
11 × 2 = 22
11 × 3 = 33
11 × 4 = 44
11 × 5 = 55
11 × 6 = 66
11 × 7 = 77
11 × 8 = 88
11 × 9 = 99
11 × 10 = 110
11 × 11 = 121
11 × 12 = 132

## 12 ×

12 × 1 = 12
12 × 2 = 24
12 × 3 = 36
12 × 4 = 48
12 × 5 = 60
12 × 6 = 72
12 × 7 = 84
12 × 8 = 96
12 × 9 = 108
12 × 10 = 120
12 × 11 = 132
12 × 12 = 144

**All the times tables up to 12 can be arranged together in a grid, known as a multiplication square.**

Choose a factor along the top and a factor down the left-hand side.

I choose 7.

Go down the column and go right along the row. Where the two meet you'll find the product!

| × | 1 | 2 | 3 | 4 | 5 | 6 | 7 | 8 | 9 | 10 | 11 | 12 |
|---|---|---|---|---|---|---|---|---|---|----|----|----|
| 1 | 1 | 2 | 3 | 4 | 5 | 6 | 7 | 8 | 9 | 10 | 11 | 12 |
| 2 | 2 | 4 | 6 | 8 | 10 | 12 | 14 | 16 | 18 | 20 | 22 | 24 |
| 3 | 3 | 6 | 9 | 12 | 15 | 18 | 21 | 24 | 27 | 30 | 33 | 36 |
| 4 | 4 | 8 | 12 | 16 | 20 | 24 | 28 | 32 | 36 | 40 | 44 | 48 |
| 5 | 5 | 10 | 15 | 20 | 25 | 30 | 35 | 40 | 45 | 50 | 55 | 60 |
| 6 | 6 | 12 | 18 | 24 | 30 | 36 | 42 | 48 | 54 | 60 | 66 | 72 |
| 7 | 7 | 14 | 21 | 28 | 35 | 42 | 49 | 56 | 63 | 70 | 77 | 84 |
| 8 | 8 | 16 | 24 | 32 | 40 | 48 | 56 | 64 | 72 | 80 | 88 | 96 |
| 9 | 9 | 18 | 27 | 36 | 45 | 54 | 63 | 72 | 81 | 90 | 99 | 108 |
| 10 | 10 | 20 | 30 | 40 | 50 | 60 | 70 | 80 | 90 | 100 | 110 | 120 |
| 11 | 11 | 22 | 33 | 44 | 55 | 66 | 77 | 88 | 99 | 110 | 121 | 132 |
| 12 | 12 | 24 | 36 | 48 | 60 | 72 | 84 | 96 | 108 | 120 | 132 | 144 |

And I choose 8.

They meet at 56.

$7 \times 8 = 56$

**You can look up divisions on the multiplication square too.**

$63 \div 9 =$ ☆

Go down the 9 column until you reach 63.

Then go left to the end of that row to find the answer.

It's 7.

Have a go at solving these multiplications and divisions.

**A**

$6 \times \bigstar = 54$

**B**

$132 \div 11 = \bigstar$

**C**

$\bigstar \div 4 = 9$

**D**

A muffin tray holds 12 muffins.

I need 144 muffins. How many trayfuls is that?

If you like a challenge, here are a couple of trickier ones!

**E**

Oranges are "buy three, get one free" and slug wants 12 oranges.

How many do I need to pay for?

**F**

What number is beetle thinking of?

It's between 20 and 25. It's odd and you can divide it by 3.

# Fractions

A fraction is a **part** of something.
You make fractions by splitting something into **equal** parts.

If you split something into **two** equal parts, each part is one **half**.

Half

If you split something into **three** equal parts, each part is one **third**.

Third

And if you split something into **four** equal parts, each part is one **quarter**.

Quarter

You can have a fraction of a shape...

A quarter of a circle.

a fraction of a length...

My wings are half as long as yours.

...and a fraction of a group.

There's one third of us in the boat.

Can you see what fractions are shown here?

One quarter.

START

One half.

One third.

# You can write fractions using maths symbols.

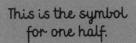

This is the symbol for one half.

The bottom number tells you how many equal parts something has been divided into.

The top number tells you how many parts you have.

$\frac{1}{2}$

This is the symbol for one third.

$\frac{1}{3}$

And this is the symbol for one quarter.

I've got one of two equal parts.

And I've got the other one.

$\frac{1}{4}$

## What fraction of each shape is shaded in?

$\frac{1}{3}$

One third.

$\frac{1}{4}$

One quarter.

$\frac{1}{2}$

One half.

## Which cucumber has been split in half?

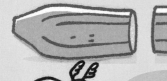

This one!

It can't be this one.

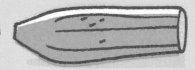

The two parts aren't equal.

# To find a fraction of a **number**, split it into smaller, equal **numbers**.

## To find a half of a number, split it into two equal parts.

We're splitting 16 beads into 2 equal groups.

That makes 8 in each group.

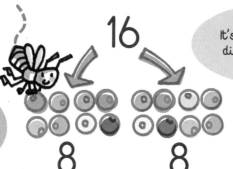

**16**

8    8

It's the same as dividing by 2.

$16 \div 2 = 8$

## To find a quarter of a number, split it into four equal parts.

Or you could split it in half, then split each half in half again.

4    4    4    4

It's the same as dividing by 4.

$16 \div 4 = 4$

Can you find $\frac{1}{3}$ of 18?

**18**

Let's make 3 equal groups.

6    6    6

It's the same as dividing by 3.

$18 \div 3 = 6$

So $\frac{1}{3}$ of 18 is 6.

## Can you solve these fraction puzzles?

**A**

$\frac{1}{2}$ of 30 = ☆

**B** A popcorn bag holds 40 pieces.

I've eaten a quarter.

POPCORN

How many pieces does slug have left?

# You can have more than one share or fraction of something.

This pie is divided into 3 equal slices...

...and I've got 2 of them!

Bee has **two thirds** of the pie. Here's how you write that as a symbol.

$\frac{2}{3}$

**Two quarters** of this flag are shaded in. How can you write that with digits?

$\frac{2}{4}$

The 2 goes on top...

...and a 4 for quarters goes on the bottom.

It's the same as a half!

$\frac{2}{4} = \frac{1}{2}$

How much of the wall has bug painted?

Three quarters!

$\frac{3}{4}$

**C** How much of the tart have the bugs eaten?

**D** Snail gave away $\frac{2}{3}$ of his cards.

I've got 2 cards left.

How many did he start with?

ANSWERS: A. 15, B. 30, C. $\frac{3}{4}$, D. 6.

45

# Measuring

You measure things to find out about their size or amount.

Here are some of the different measurements you can make.

## LENGTH

How long are the sleeves?

## HEIGHT

How tall am I?

Length, height and width all measure **distance**.

## WIDTH

How wide is the doorway?

Will the table fit through?

## TEMPERATURE

How hot is it today?

## CAPACITY

Capacity measures the **space inside** something.

How much water does this jug hold?

## VOLUME

Volume measures the space something takes up.

How many blocks is this cube made of?

46

# PERIMETER

Perimeter is the **distance around the edge** of something.

How many bricks do I need to make a fence?

# AREA

Area is the **space inside a flat shape**.

How many brownie squares cover the bottom of this tray?

# MASS and WEIGHT

Mass and weight both measure how **heavy** something is.

Mass is **how much stuff** something's made up of.

Weight measures the **force** pulling down on something.

How heavy is the parcel?

In space, there's less pulling force. The parcel's **mass** stays the same...

...but its **weight** is much less.

# TIME

What's the time please?

When do the holidays start?

How long did I take?

0:57

AUGUST

# You can measure something by comparing it with something else.

To compare heights, you need to arrange things so they're all starting on the same level.

To compare lengths, you need to arrange things so their ends all line up.

You can also measure things using numbers.
To do this, you have to measure in set amounts, called **units**.

You can make units out of anything.

But if your units don't match someone else's, things can go wrong...

The recipe said we needed a cup of water.

Oh no, I used the wrong type of cup!

To avoid getting in a muddle, people use amounts called **standard units**.
These are the same all around the world.

# EXAMPLES OF STANDARD UNITS

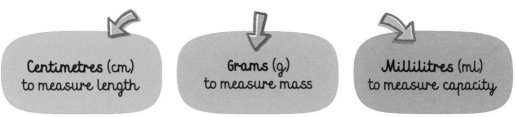

Centimetres (cm) to measure length

Grams (g) to measure mass

Millilitres (ml) to measure capacity

To measure things in standard units, you use different tools or pieces of equipment.

The tools have little marks and numbers on them, known as **scales**.

Each scale starts at zero, then counts up in standard units.

This weighing scale measures grams.

This jug measures millilitres.

This measuring tape measures centimetres.

# To measure the **length**, **height** or **width** of something, you measure the distance from one end to the other.

Here's how you measure a box.

I'm measuring the width.

We're measuring the length.

I'm measuring the height.

For each measurement, line your ruler up with the edge of the box. Make sure the zero is at the start of the side.

Read the number where the ruler reaches the other side of the box.

## Use the ruler along the side of this page to measure some of the things around you.

The numbers tell you the length in centimetres.

If the numbers or lines don't line up exactly with what you're measuring, choose the nearest one.

How long is your longest finger, in centimetres?

The little lines show millimetres.

There are 10 millimetres in a centimetre.

Always start measuring from zero.

How wide is your smallest fingernail in millimetres?

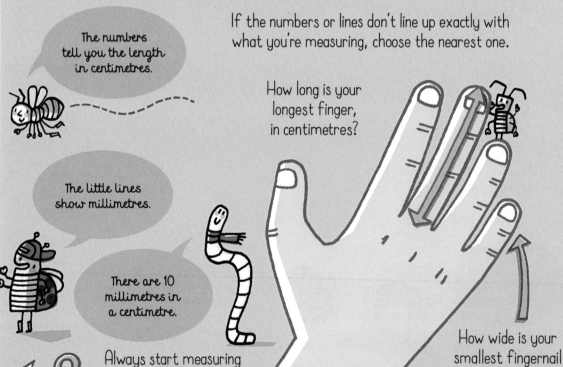

20 19 18 17 16 15 14 13 12 11 10 9 8 7 6 5 4 3 2 1 0 cm

**You can measure very short distances and very long ones, such as...**

The length of a leaf

The height of a building

The distance to the Moon

You use **millimetres** (mm) to measure tiny things.

You use **centimetres** (cm) to measure small things.

The stalk is 7 mm long.

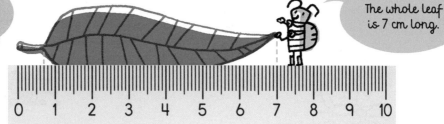

The whole leaf is 7 cm long.

For longer distances, you can use **metres** (m).

There are 100 centimetres in a metre.

9 m

For very long distances, you can use **kilometres** (km).

There are 1,000 metres in a kilometre.

BUGVILLE 1 km

**What units would you use to measure across these things?**

A  A field

B  An ocean

C  A precious jewel

ANSWERS: A. metres, B. kilometres, C. millimetres.

# The distance around something is called its **perimeter**.

To find the perimeter of a shape, you can measure the length of each side and add them all up.

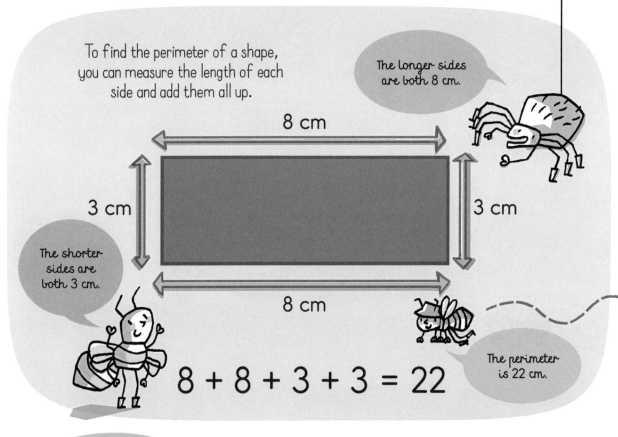

The longer sides are both 8 cm.

8 cm

3 cm

3 cm

The shorter sides are both 3 cm.

8 cm

The perimeter is 22 cm.

$$8 + 8 + 3 + 3 = 22$$

How far has grasshopper jogged?

I've just jogged around this football pitch.

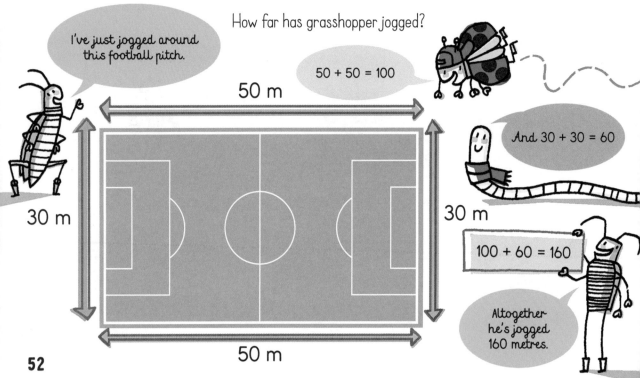

50 + 50 = 100

50 m

30 m

30 m

And 30 + 30 = 60

100 + 60 = 160

50 m

Altogether he's jogged 160 metres.

52

# The space inside a flat shape is called its **area**.

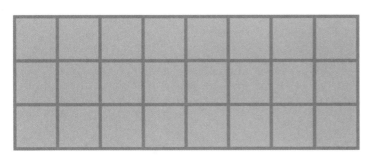

This shape is made up of squares. To find out the area, you can count the squares.

There are 24 altogether.

You can use multiplication to find out the area of this shape.

There are 3 rows of 8 squares.

$3 \times 8 = 24$ **squares**

## Count the squares to compare the areas of these shapes.

Which shape has the **biggest** area?

It's the one with the **most** squares.

Which shape has the **smallest** area?

It's the one with the **least** squares.

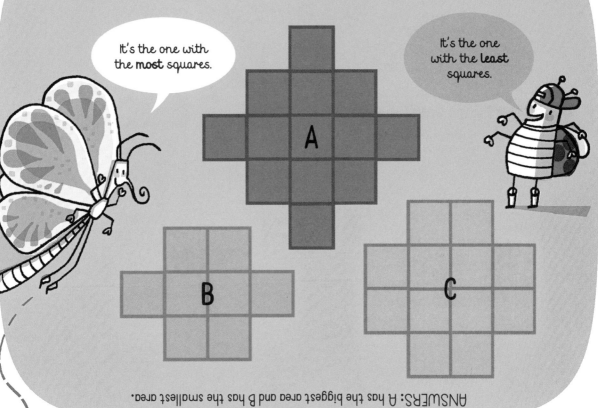

ANSWERS: A has the biggest area and B has the smallest area.

53

# You weigh things to measure how heavy they are.

Guess which of these is the heaviest.

Feather

Pebble

Which is the lightest?

The pebble!

The feather.

Twig

## The more you have of the same thing, the heavier it becomes.

There are more of us, so we're weighing down this side of the seesaw.

## But bigger things aren't always heavier than smaller things.

A small tin of beans is heavier than a big beach ball.

It depends what each thing is made of and what they're filled with.

The tin has more mass.

## Should I say mass or weight?

In everyday life, people say weight instead of mass and that's fine.
But in maths and science, the correct term is mass.

# Mass is measured in grams (g) and kilograms (kg).

Use grams to measure lighter things...

...and kilograms to measure heavier things.

There are 1,000 grams in a kilogram.

80 g

Sugar

1 kg

## It can be useful to have a rough idea of how much things weigh.

Here are some things that weigh roughly 1 g.

$1

These things all weigh roughly 1 kg.

Which is heavier, a kilogram of feathers or a kilogram of rocks?

Neither! They both weigh 1 kilogram.

Would you measure these things in grams or kilograms?

A  A person

B  Ball of wool

C  Teddy bear

ANSWERS: A. kilograms, B. & C. grams

# The amount that a container can hold is called its **capacity**.

Which can hold more tea?

Teapot

Teacup

The teapot. It has a bigger capacity than the teacup.

Which has the smallest capacity?

Swimming pool

Paddling pool

The paddling pool. It holds less water.

How much of the container's capacity is filled?

All of it. It's full.

Now it's half full.

Or half empty.

And now it's empty! None of its capacity is filled.

## You can measure capacity using cubes.

Count up the sugar cubes to work out the capacity of each box.

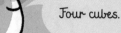

Four cubes.

Six cubes.

If you're measuring liquids, you can use **millilitres (ml)** and **litres (l)**.

You use millilitres for small amounts.

There are 1,000 millilitres in a litre.

This cylinder has a capacity of 100 ml.

We've added 30 ml of water.

You use litres for larger amounts.

This water butt can hold 100 litres.

It's half full, so that's 50 litres of rainwater!

100
90
80
70
60
50
40
30
20
10 ml

When you next go shopping, try looking at the unit of measurement on things. What units do you think these items are usually measured in?

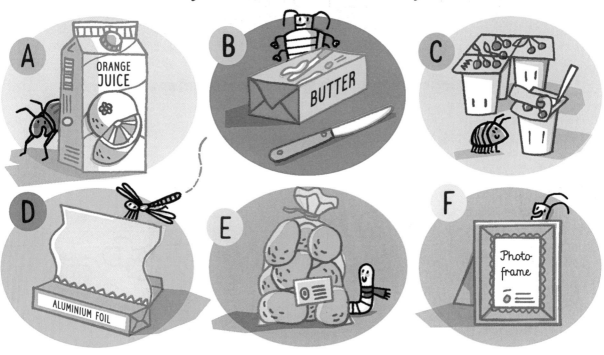

A   ORANGE JUICE

B   BUTTER

C

D   ALUMINIUM FOIL

E

F   Photo frame

ANSWERS: A. litres, B. grams, C. millilitres or grams, D. metres, E. kilograms, F. centimetres

57

# Telling the time

Time tells us when things happen and how long they take.

There are words for different days...

I went to the dentist's **yesterday**.

I'm at the dentist's **today**.

I'm going to the dentist's **tomorrow**.

...and words for different times of day.

Good morning.

Good afternoon.

Good evening.

Good night.

## The units for measuring time are **seconds**, **minutes** and **hours**.

A second lasts roughly as long as it takes you to say...

Wait a second!

There are 60 seconds in a minute.

That's about how long you need to take 10 deep breaths.

There are 60 minutes in an hour.

It takes about an hour to bake a fruit cake.

Try counting slowly in seconds. 1... 2... 3... 4...

What else can you do in one minute?

And there are 24 hours in a day.

# Clocks, watches and screens show us the time in two main ways.

## Digital clocks use digits.

The number before the dots tells you the hour.

The number after the dots tells you the minutes past the hour.

AM means **before** midday. PM means **after midday.**

## Traditional clocks have pointers called **hands.**

Each number shows an hour of the day.

The **short hand** points to the **hour.**

Long hand

Short hand

The minutes are marked by little lines.

The **long hand** shows how many **minutes** have gone by in each hour (see page 60).

The hands move this way. It's called clockwise.

# You can divide each hour into quarters and halves.

If the long hand is pointing to the 12, then it's something **o'clock.**

O'clock

The short hand is pointing to 1, so it's 1 o'clock.

Here, the long hand has gone a quarter of the way around.

Quarter past

It's quarter past 1.

How far around has the long hand gone here?

Half past

Half way. It's half past one.

Now there's only a quarter of the way to go to reach the top again.

Quarter to

At the top it will be 2 o'clock. So it's a quarter to 2 now.

# You can tell the time by counting minutes.
# There are minutes **past** the hour and minutes **to** the next hour.

It takes 5 minutes for the long hand to move from one number to the next.

Try counting up in fives. If the long hand is on 4, then count 5, 10, 15, 20 – it's 20 minutes past the hour.

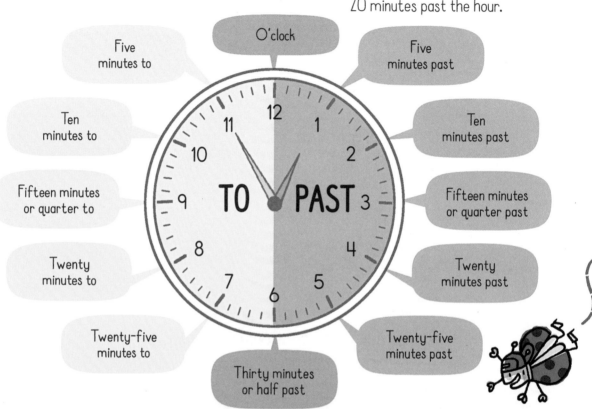

O'clock

Five minutes to

Five minutes past

Ten minutes to

Ten minutes past

Fifteen minutes or quarter to

Fifteen minutes or quarter past

Twenty minutes to

Twenty minutes past

Twenty-five minutes to

Twenty-five minutes past

Thirty minutes or half past

TO   PAST

## What are the times on these clocks?

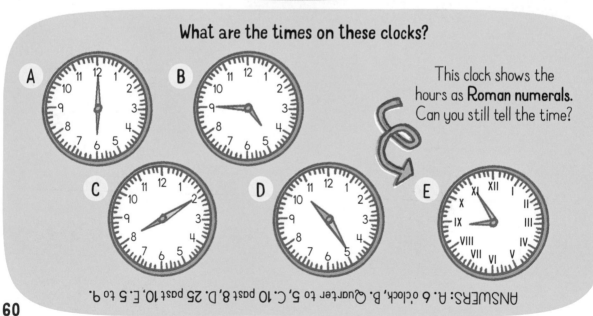

A

B

This clock shows the hours as **Roman numerals**. Can you still tell the time?

C

D

E

ANSWERS: A, 6 o'clock, B, Quarter to 5, C, 10 past 8, D, 25 past 10, E, 5 to 9.

Longer periods of time are measured in **days**, **weeks**, **months** and even **years**.

There are 7 **days** in a week. Here they are in order.

Monday    Tuesday    Wednesday    Thursday    Friday    Saturday    Sunday

There are 52 weeks in a year.

YEAR PLANNER

These two days make up the weekend.

Each year is split into 12 **months**.

| January | February | March | April |
|---|---|---|---|
| May | June | July | August |
| September | October | November | December |

Each month is made up of about 30 days. You number the days to give exact **dates**.

AUGUST
14

This date is the 14th of August.

Here's a way to remember the exact number of days in each month, using your knuckles and the gaps in between.

The months ON the knuckles have 31 days...

JAN    FEB    MAR    APR    MAY    JUN    JUL    AUG    SEP    OCT    NOV    DEC

February has 28 days most years, and 29 in a leap year...

...and the rest have 30 days.

Which date comes after this one?

Wednesday
30th
APRIL

ANSWER: Thursday 1st May

Which day comes before this one?

Monday
1st
AUGUST

ANSWER: Sunday 31st July

# Money

## You use money to pay for things. Money comes in coins and notes.

The number on a coin or note tells you its value – how much it's worth.

My coin is worth 10 of beetle's coin.

My coin has the lowest value.

Notes are usually worth more than coins.

You can also pay for things with credit cards or with your phone.

## Different countries use different **units** of money.

Here are some of the units and their symbols.

**£** Pounds ⟹ **p** Pennies

A **pound** is made up of 100 **pennies**.

**$** Dollars ⟹ **¢** Cents

A **dollar** is made up of 100 **cents**.

**€** Euros ⟹ **c** Cents

A **euro** is made up of 100 **cents**.

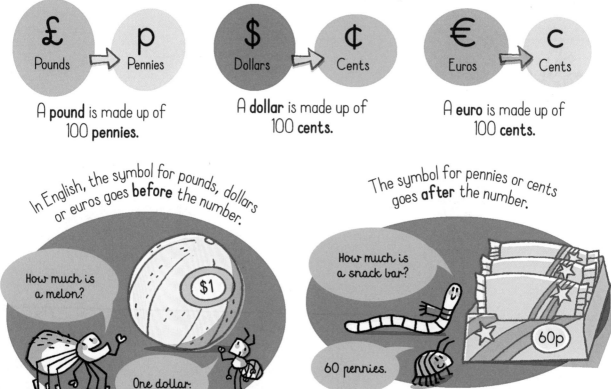

In English, the symbol for pounds, dollars or euros goes **before** the number.

The symbol for pennies or cents goes **after** the number.

How much is a melon?

One dollar.

How much is a snack bar?

60 pennies.

In other languages, the € often goes after the number.

# You can combine coins to make all kinds of amounts.

Here are some of the ways you can make 20p.

Use **addition** to work out the total value of the coins.

10 + 10 = 20

## If a drink costs one dollar, which combination of these coins could you use?

Remember, a dollar is 100 cents, so the numbers on the coins need to add up to 100...

Let's start with the higher value coins.

We still need another 25.

Let's add two 10¢ coins and a 5¢.

$1

3 x 25 = 75

25¢ + 25¢ + 25¢ + 10¢ + 10¢ + 5¢ = ○ $1 ○

# When you go shopping, you'll see prices written like this.

£2.99

2 pounds....

...and 99 pennies.

A small dot separates the two.
It's called a **decimal point**.

$3.75

3 dollars...

...and 75 cents.

€1.20

1 euro...

...and 20 cents.

How much does this shopping add up to?

Add the cents first.

$$20 + 70 = 90$$

90 cents.

Then add on the euros.

There are 2 euros and 90 cents.

€2.90

€1.20
Sandwich

70c

€1

Spider has ordered a fruit smoothie and a slice of pizza.
How much will that cost?

## MENU

Orange juice - £1.50

Fruit smoothie - £2.60

Pizza slice - £2.25

Pasta - £3.50

BILL
£4.85

That's 4 pounds and 85 pennies, please.

## If you don't have the exact money, the shopkeeper or waiter can give you change.

Change is the **difference** between the money paid and the price.

You can write it as a **subtraction**.

MONEY PAID - PRICE = CHANGE

Spider pays for his pizza and smoothie with a £5 note. How much change does he get?

BILL

£4.85

o £5 o

£5 - £4.85 = ⭐

An easy way to work this out is to **count on** from the price until you reach the amount paid.

Here's 10p. That makes £4.95.

And 5p more makes £5.

10p

5p

10p + 5p = 15p

I get 15p change.

## Can you solve these puzzles?

**A**

Bee has a 10 euro note.

She buys a scarf that costs 8 euros.

How much change does she get?

**B**

Beetle has these coins in his purse.

50p  20p
20p  5p  1p

Can I buy any sandwich or roll I like?

Cheese 80p

Tuna 95p

Chicken £1.10

ANSWERS: A. €2, B. No, only the cheese or tuna ones.

# Shapes

There are all kinds of different shapes. Some are flat and some are solid.

In maths, flat shapes are called **2D**.
They have different numbers of **edges** and **corners**.

Edge

Corner

A corner is where two or more edges meet.

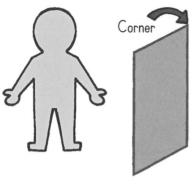

Corner

Another word for a corner is a **vertex**. For more than one, you say **vertices**.

Some shapes are **symmetrical**.
This means one half is an exact reflection of the other.

I'm symmetrical!

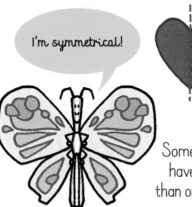

The line between the two halves is called a **line of symmetry**.

Some shapes have more than one line of symmetry.

Try cutting out different shapes from a piece of paper, then folding them in half.

## What does 2D mean?

It means that a shape has 2 dimensions – or 2 directions you can measure it in.

A line only has 1 dimension.

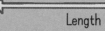

Length

A flat shape has 2 dimensions. It's **2D**.

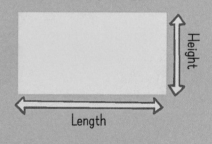

Height

Length

A solid shape has 3 dimensions. It's **3D**.

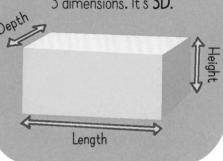

Depth

Height

Length

If the halves match up exactly, then the shape is symmetrical.

Lots of shapes have their own names.

# TRIANGLES

These all have 3 edges and 3 corners.

# PENTAGONS

These all have 5 edges and 5 corners.

# RECTANGLES

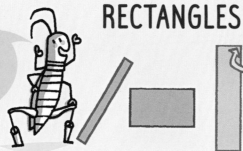

These all have 4 corners and 4 edges. The opposite edges are the same length.

The 4 corners are all the same shape. This kind of corner is called a **right angle**.

**Regular shapes** are shapes where all the edges and all the corners are equal.

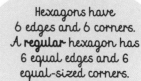

Regular triangle

Regular pentagon

Regular hexagon

Hexagons have 6 edges and 6 corners. A **regular** hexagon has 6 equal edges and 6 equal-sized corners.

A regular rectangle is called a square!

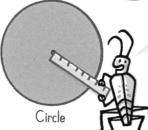

Square

Circle

All circles are regular. The edge is always the same distance from the middle.

# Here are some examples of 3D shapes.

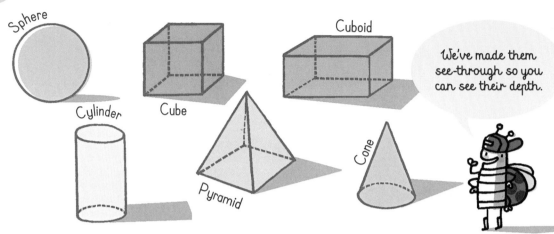

Sphere

Cube

Cuboid

We've made them see-through so you can see their depth.

Cylinder

Pyramid

Cone

Can you spot these 3D shapes in your home?

I've got lots of cylinders.

A ball is a sphere.

Here are some cuboids.

Dice are cubes.

I've found a cone!

Try pushing a 3D shape and see what happens.

Curved ones roll...

...and flat ones slide!

Which shapes are these objects?

A

B

C

ANSWERS: A. Cylinder, B. Cone, C. Cuboid

68

# The words you use to describe and compare shapes are called **properties**.

On 3D shapes you can count **faces**, as well as edges and corners.

Cubes and cuboids have 6 faces.

Top

4 around the sides

Bottom

Remember to include the faces you can't see around the back.

A cylinder has 3 faces.

Top

1 curving all around the middle

Bottom

GLUE

GLUE

## Compare the properties of these 3D shapes.

| SHAPE | EDGES | CORNERS | FACES |
|---|---|---|---|
| CUBE / CUBOID | 12 | 8 | 6 |
| SPHERE | 0 | 0 | 1 |
| CYLINDER | 2 | 0 | 3 |
| SQUARE-BASED PYRAMID | 8 | 5 | 5 |
| CONE | 1 | 1 | 2 |

Many 3D shapes have at least one flat side. If you use them as stamps, what 2D shapes can you make?

A square.

A rectangle or a square.

Circles!

A triangle or a square.

# Position and direction

There are lots of useful words to describe where things are and which way they're going.

I'm at the **top**.

I'm at the **far away**.

I'm **outside**.

I'm in the **middle**.

I'm **inside**.

And I'm at the **bottom**.

I'm **between** two posts.

I'm **near** the sandpit.

I'm going **forwards**.

I'm going **backwards**.

Which directions are these bugs going in?

I'm going **straight on**.

I've turned **left**.

I've turned **right**.

# There are also useful words to describe **turning**.

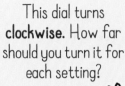

This dial turns **clockwise**. How far should you turn it for each setting?

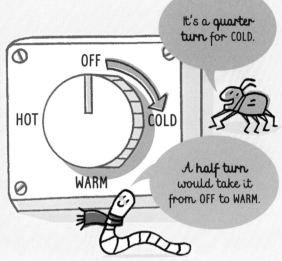

OFF

HOT

COLD

WARM

It's a **quarter turn** for COLD.

You can also call a quarter turn a **right angle**.

If you turn the dial from OFF all the way around to OFF again, that's a **whole turn**.

A **half turn** would take it from OFF to WARM.

A **three-quarter turn** would take it to HOT.

Can you copy ladybird and make these turns yourself?

START

Quarter turn right

Half turn left

Three-quarter turn right

Whole turn either way

## Ant is lost in a maze. Can you guide her to the exit?

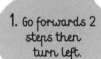

Each square is one step.

Try turning the book after each direction, so you're facing the same way as ant.

1. Go forwards 2 steps then turn left.

2. Go straight on for 3 steps, then turn left again.

3. Go forwards 4 steps, then make a quarter turn to your right.

EXIT

4. The exit is straight ahead!

# Patterns and sequences

You can put shapes together in a special order to make a **sequence**.
And you can repeat a sequence to make a **pattern**.

The order here is yellow square, blue square.

To continue the pattern, what colour will the next square be?

Blue!

This pattern has a sequence of three shapes that's repeated.

To continue the pattern, what comes next?

A yellow rectangle.

## Can you solve these puzzles?

**A** Which bug is missing from this pattern?

**B** Where will the arrow point next?

The arrow moves a quarter turn clockwise each time...

ANSWERS: A. Spider, B. Down

72

# You can make sequences with numbers too.

To understand a sequence, you need to work out the rules or ideas behind it.
What's the rule here?

**Each ladybird has 2 more spots than the one before.**

Who comes next?

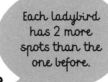

**Me! I've got 10 spots.**

## What's happening with this sequence?

| 17 | 15 | 13 | 11 | 9 | 7 |
|----|----|----|----|---|---|

−2   −2

**The colour is switching between yellow and green.**

**And the number is going down 2 each time.**

What comes next?

**7 − 2 = 5**

**It's a 5 on a yellow rectangle!**

# Fly is making a sequence using shapes, sizes and colours.

Compare each shape with the next.
Which one thing does fly change each time?

It's got bigger.

Now it's a triangle.

It's changed colour.

Now it's got smaller.

**I can go back to the small yellow square now and repeat the sequence!**

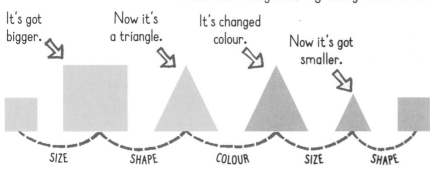

SIZE   SHAPE   COLOUR   SIZE   SHAPE

# Have a go at making your own sequence.

You could use shapes or numbers.

Think what your rule is. What's changing each time?

Show your sequence to a friend. Can they work out what comes next?

# Using data

**Data** is a collection of facts. You can use data to find out useful information.

Here are some examples of when data can be useful.

Which fruit shall we buy for the players?

Let's ask everyone what they like best.

How busy is the road by the park?

Let's see how many vehicles go by in an hour.

Should I pack a coat?

Let's check what the weather forecast is for next week.

You can collect data by talking to others...

Which fruit do you like best?

...or by looking and counting.

I'm counting the different vehicles going by.

Information stored or used on a computer or smart phone is also called **data**.

# Tallying is useful for keeping track of counting.

This **tally chart** shows which fruits the players like best.
There were 24 players altogether, and they each chose one type of fruit.

| FRUIT | HOW MANY CHOSE IT |
|---|---|
| Apples | 卌 |
| Bananas | 卌 I |
| Oranges | II |
| Mangoes | III |
| Strawberries | 卌 III |

Each little mark represents a player.

If someone says a new fruit, you can add it here.

For more on tally marks, turn back to page 7.

## You could then show the same information on a chart called a **pictogram**.

A pictogram uses pictures or symbols to represent the data.

On this pictogram, each picture represents a player who chose that fruit.

| FRUIT | HOW MANY CHOSE IT |
|---|---|
| Apples | 🍎🍎🍎🍎🍎 |
| Bananas | 🍌🍌🍌🍌🍌🍌 |
| Oranges | 🍊🍊 |
| Mangoes | 🥭🥭🥭 |
| Strawberries | 🍓🍓🍓🍓🍓🍓🍓🍓 |

The fruit with the longest line of pictures is the most popular.

Which fruit is the least popular?

Oranges!

## A simple way to present data is in a **table**.

This table shows the vehicles beetle counted.

Make sure the table is neat, so the information is easy to read.

| VEHICLE TYPE | HOW MANY |
| --- | --- |
| Car | 6 |
| Truck | 2 |
| Bike | 2 |
| Bus | 1 |
| Motorbike | 4 |

It's often easier to **compare facts** when you see them on a **chart** or a **graph**.

You can take the data from a table and turn it into a **block graph**.

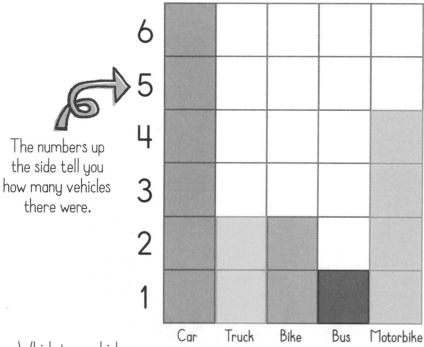

The numbers up the side tell you how many vehicles there were.

Each block represents one vehicle.

There's a different colour for each type of vehicle.

Which two vehicles appeared the most?

Cars and motorbikes.

How could you make the road less busy?

Go by bus or walk instead of driving!

**When you're dealing with larger amounts, a bar chart can be useful.**

The bugs held a vote to decide which 3 events to have on their sports day. They could only vote for one event each.

The bars represent the events. The top of each bar lines up with the number of bugs who voted for it.

How many chose the obstacle race? I'll follow this line to find out... The answer is 8.

NUMBER OF BUGS

EVENTS

Skipping    Egg & spoon    Sack race    Tug of war    Obstacle race

**Can you use the data above to answer these questions?**

**A** Which 3 events were the **most** popular?

**B** Which event was the **least** popular?

**C** How many **more** bugs voted for the sack race than for skipping?

**D** How many bugs voted **altogether**?

ANSWERS: A. Sack race, egg & spoon and obstacle race, B. Skipping, C. 11, D. 39

77

# Glossary

Here you can look up the meanings of some of the maths words in this book.

**2D** – having only two dimensions: length and height. Flat shapes are 2D.

**3D** – having three dimensions: length, height and depth. Solid shapes are 3D.

**Anti-clockwise** – moving in the opposite direction to the hands of a clock.

**Area** – the space inside a flat shape.

**Bar chart** – a way of presenting data using bars of different heights to represent different amounts.

**Block graph** – a way of presenting data using stacks of blocks to represent different amounts.

**Capacity** – the space inside a 3D shape.

**Clockwise** – moving in the same direction as the hands of a clock.

**Cuboid** – a 3D shape with 6 rectangular faces, where all the corners are right-angles.

**Data** – a collection of facts.

**Digits** – the number symbols 0 to 9, either on their own or put together to make larger numbers.

**Dividing** – sharing equally.

**Even** – describes numbers that you can divide exactly by two.

**Faces** – the different surfaces on a 3D shape.

**Fact family** – a group of maths questions and answers, all based on the same numbers.

**Fraction** – a part of a whole or of a group of things, e.g. a half.

**Hexagon** – a flat shape with 6 straight edges and 6 corners.

**Multiplying** – adding a number to itself one or more times, or enlarging the size of something.

**Number bonds** – pairs of numbers that add up to the same total.

**Odd** – describes numbers that you can't divide exactly by two.

**Partitioning** – splitting a number up, so you write out the ones, tens and hundreds separately.

**Pentagon** – a flat shape with 5 straight edges and 5 corners.

**Perimeter** – the distance around all the edges of a flat shape.

**Pictogram** – a chart that uses pictures or symbols to represent data.

**Properties** – qualities you can use to describe and compare things, for example the number of edges or faces in a shape.

**Regular shape** – a shape with equal edges and equal sized corners.

**Right-angle** – the shape of a corner in a square or rectangle. It's the same as a quarter turn.

**Rounding** – adjusting a number to make a calculation easier. Rounding up makes a number higher, rounding down makes it lower.

**Sphere** – a perfectly round ball. Every point on its surface is an equal distance from its centre.

**Subtracting** – taking away one number from another, or comparing two numbers to find the difference.

**Tally marks** – lines used for counting, usually drawn in groups of five.

**Units** – set amounts for measuring things, such as centimetres for length or grams for mass.

**Volume** – the space a solid, 3D shape takes up.

# Index

Use this index to find out which pages things are mentioned on.

Things are listed in alphabetical order, from A to W. (There aren't any Xs, Ys or Zs).

First published in 2021 by Usborne Publishing Ltd., Usborne House, 83-85 Saffron Hill, London EC1N 8RT, England.
usborne.com Copyright © 2021 Usborne Publishing Ltd. The name Usborne and the balloon logos are Trade Marks of Usborne Publishing Ltd.